Taming the Tiger
How to Heal Your Past
with EMDR Therapy

Taming the Tiger
How to Heal Your Past
with EMDR Therapy

Mark Odland - MA, LMFT, MDIV

Bilateral Innovations
Minnesota

Published in the United States by Bilateral Innovations

Names: Odland, Mark, author.
Title: Taming the Tiger - How to Heal Your Past with EMDR Therapy
Description: First American edition. Minnesota: Bilateral Innovations, an assumed name of North Woods Christian Counseling, LLC, [2019]
BISAC 1: Nonfiction / Self Help / Posttraumatic Stress Disorder
BISAC 2: Nonfiction / Psychology / Mental Health

ISBN: 9781091292109

Content available as a Book, eBook, AudioBook, and Online Course

PRINTED IN THE UNITED STATES OF AMERICA
10 9 8 7 6 5 4 3 2 1

First American Edition

ACKNOWLEDGEMENTS

I could not have written a book like this without crediting the inventor of EMDR therapy, Francine Shapiro. Her innovation and persistence in developing this groundbreaking therapy has transformed the lives of millions. I highly recommend that you read her book *Getting Past Your Past: Take Control of Your Life with Self-Help Techniques from EMDR Therapy*. It will not only provide you with practical tools for emotional regulation, but will also take you into an even deeper understanding of yourself, of EMDR therapy, and how it can improve your life.

Taming the Tiger: How to Heal Your Past with EMDR Therapy is written in the same spirit, and is intended to offer the public a brief, accessible introduction EMDR. My hope is that it will complement Dr. Shapiro's work, fulfilling the same purpose of educating the world about the healing power of EMDR therapy.

Whenever possible, in this book I cite my sources to give credit where it is due. However, as an EMDR Therapist I've attended dozens of trainings, and over time have been blessed to glean wisdom from many talented clinicians along the way. If there are ever places in this book where someone is not properly credited, it is only because these pearls of wisdom have blended together over time. When in doubt, it should be assumed that the credit goes back to Dr. Shapiro herself.

Of course, as with all my creative endeavors, I have to also thank my wife Rachel for being such a steady reminder of what is good and true in this world... inspiring me, supporting me, and pointing me back to the things that matter most in life.

I'd like to conclude these acknowledgments by thanking you, the reader. I'm honored that you chose to invest in this book, and I hope that it plays some small role in your journey towards hope and healing.

Sincerely,

Mark Odland

CONTENTS

CHAPTER 1
THE POWER OF EMDR THERAPY

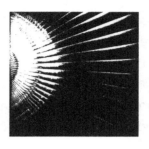

Introduction

We live in a world ripped apart by trauma. Just turn on the news, and there it is. Another war, another attack, another epidemic. And even if we turn off the news, we're still left with the reality of our own lives and the challenges within our own families. Illness, death, broken relationships... and then there's our regrets... our doubts... our insecurities, and our fears... all amplified by unhealed wounds from the past. So often, we try to ignore these wounds. But over time, it catches up with us. Whether we like to admit it or not, our past shapes us. It shapes not only how we see the world, it literally changes our brains.

From 1995-1997 Kaiser Permanente did a massive study of over 17,000 subjects to try and better understand the way trauma experienced in childhood impacted individuals long-term. In what is now known as the (ACE) study, because it focused on

"Adverse Childhood Experiences," subjects completed confidential surveys, allowing researchers to gather data on their experiences of physical, sexual, and emotional abuse; emotional and physical neglect; and negative household experiences like divorce, addiction, violence and incarceration... and the results were jaw-dropping.[1]

The researchers found that not only were these adverse childhood experiences very common, but that as the number of these experiences increased, so did the individual's risk for a whole host of problems later in life. One might expect that there would be some mental health issues because of childhood pain... but the study demonstrated that the damage was even more pervasive. In fact, showed a direct link between these painful experiences and an increased likelihood of having medical and socio-economic problems later in life... like addiction, heart disease, liver disease, financial stress, academic problems, risky behaviors, suicide attempts, and domestic violence.[2]

One of the big confirmations from this study was the importance of not only trying to minimize and prevent these painful experiences from happening, but also... (here's where EMDR comes in)... also trying to heal the emotional trauma so that these

---

[1] Centers for Disease Control and Prevention website, https://www.cdc.gov/violenceprevention/acestudy/index.html.

[2] Centers for Disease Control and Prevention website, https://www.cdc.gov/violenceprevention/acestudy/index.html.

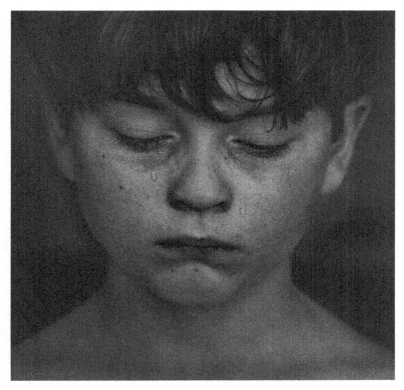

"...our past shapes us"

problems later in life don't have to manifest the same way. Yes, there is a silver lining in all this. There is a ray of light in the midst of so much darkness in this world. With EMDR therapy, trauma <u>can</u> permanently heal, allowing individuals to live healthier, more joyful lives, and eventually break the destructive patterns passed down from generation to generation. In this sense, EMDR truly can change the world! And I'm so honored to tell you about it.

My name is Mark Odland, and I'd like to personally welcome you to this crash course on EMDR therapy, and how it can transform your life! EMDR therapy is, simply put, the most groundbreaking and powerful therapy out there. Its 8 phase process is highly researched, and at the time of this publication has been empirically validated by over 2 dozen randomized studies of trauma victims. It's been recognized by the American Psychiatric Association, the Department of Veterans Affairs, and the Department of Defense. And it's also one of only two trauma therapies that have been endorsed by the World Health Organization for treating PTSD. From the outside, it can look a little too good to be true. But the research doesn't lie. EMDR is the real deal, and it's here to stay.

But to be clear, this book itself is not EMDR therapy, because EMDR is something you'd receive over the course of several weeks or months from a trained, mental health professional. This book itself isn't therapy, and it's not a quick fix. But it is an in-depth introduction to EMDR therapy. My goal is to take the mystery out of it… to pull back the curtain to show you exactly what it is, how it works, why it works, and how it can help you or someone you love find lasting healing from trauma. Knowledge is power, and my hope is that this book helps you see, and

"...memories become frozen"

believe, that emotional pain doesn't have to have the last word. That old hurts can, in fact, heal... permanently.

In our time together, you'll learn to recognize how past hurts may still be impacting your thoughts, emotions, behaviors, and relationships. And I'll teach you about the remarkable (AIP system), or Adaptive Information Processing system, the amazing process of how our brains are wired to naturally heal from emotional pain... and, how sometimes trauma overwhelms this system, causing painful memories to become dysfunctionally stored... frozen in time. And, of course, you'll learn about the power of EMDR therapy... what it is, where it came from, and how it can jump start the brain's inherent ability to once again, naturally heal itself. When this course is over, you'll leave with a better understanding of how trauma has impacted you and your loved ones, and a concrete plan for how to begin the journey toward healing.

Presenter Bio

There are plenty of EMDR therapists out there who could give you this information. However, I'm not aware of anyone else presenting all this information to the general public in such a concise way. So here I am, and I'm grateful for the chance to share this information with you. This course draws on all the education, training, and experience that I've gained over the years as a Licensed Marriage and Family Therapist, certified in EMDR. Using this powerful therapy, I've had the great privilege of helping hundreds of individuals heal from their trauma, and discover a deeper sense of peace and purpose in their lives.

I'm an LMFT and LPCC Board-Approved Supervisor for the state of Minnesota, an Approved Consultant and CE credit Provider with the EMDR International Association, and an Approved EMDR Consultant and Basic Training Facilitator with the EMDR Humanitarian Assistance Programs (EMDR HAP). In this capacity, I have the joy and honor of helping therapists around the world improve their skills. On the flip side, I've also been blessed with the opportunity to receive my own EMDR therapy, and so I know what it's like to be sitting on that couch as a client. I can honestly say that the experience transformed my life for the better. It's helped me to heal from old hurts, find deeper peace, and become a better husband, father, and therapist. I thought it was important for you to know that. That I'm not just speaking only from the perspective of a therapist, but also as someone who's been through it as a client.

In our time together I'll use short stories, humor, and metaphor to help you each step of the way. In this book, you'll not only get the head knowledge, you'll also get a glimpse of EMDR therapy in action and will leave with a concrete plan for what to do when the book is over. EMDR therapy has changed the lives of millions of people around the world… and if it's the right fit, it could change your life too. So thanks again for sharing your time with me. No pressure, no obligation… just a chance to listen, reflect, and learn more. What you choose to do with it is, of course, up to you. Let's get started!

"... it could change your life too."

What EMDR Therapy is and Where it Comes From

In 1987, Dr. Francine Shapiro was taking a walk in the park. This walk would have been like any other, but on this particular day she made the chance discovery that eye movements can reduce the intensity of disturbing thoughts. Curious, she began to study this principle and began conducting research. And only two years after that walk in the park, Dr. Shapiro was able to publish the treatment's success in the *Journal of Traumatic Stress*. Since then, the therapy has benefitted from the clinical work and research of therapists all over the world, and has been developed into a set of standardized protocols.[3]

EMDR stands for "Eye Movement Desensitization and Reprocessing." It is a kind of counseling, or psychotherapy, that helps people experience lasting healing from their emotional pain. Although it's famous for is eye movements, it can actually use several types of bilateral stimulation (which is a fancy way of saying "any left to right, back and forth stimulus"). EMDR actually has eight distinct phases and is a comprehensive approach to therapy, addressing not only one's past, but also one's present triggers and hopes for the future. To give you a thorough explanation of the process, I'll describe each of these eight phases of therapy so you can be well-informed, and have a better sense of the process. In these explanations, I'll be paraphrasing

---

[3] EMDR Institute Website, http://www.emdr.com/history-of-emdr/.

content from the EMDR International Association's website, emdria.org. But first, I'd like to give you a basic overview trauma... specifically, how it works, and how it can heal naturally with EMDR.

Why EMDR Therapy Works: The AIP System

The dozens of studies, and the millions of people who have benefitted from EMDR is proof enough that it works. So the next natural question is, "why?" Why does it work? From the outside, it seems a little too good to be true… a little too simple. But remember, EMDR is much more than moving your eyes back and forth. Again, it's an entire approach to therapy, an 8 phase standard protocol used by highly trained clinicians… a therapy that not only uses the remarkable intervention of bilateral stimulation, but is also grounded in a deep understanding of how the brain heals from trauma. To understand why EMDR works, we first need to understand how the brain works. And specifically, how the brain heals.

Dr. Shapiro's name for the brain's natural healing process is the AIP System, or the Adaptive Information Processing System. EMDR works so powerfully because it jumpstarts this system and helps the brain do what is was wired to do, heal naturally. Think about it this way… if you get a cut, the wound will naturally heal, as long as there's nothing stuck inside that will cause an infection. Some are surprised to discover that the way we heal through disturbing memories is actually very similar. In most cases, we're able to process through disturbing events, learn from them, and allow them to fade into the past as historical memories, much like that cut, healing naturally. However, sometimes an event, or series of events overwhelms the brain's ability to cope, and like an infection, slows down healing and causes pain.[4]

Decades ago, Dr. Shapiro recognized a profound truth. It was this… that the majority of our mental health symptoms are not because of an individual's character flaws, lack of willpower, or any other standard explanation. Rather, they're actually caused by dysfunctionally stored memories… memories that have for one reason or another, not been able to heal naturally the way they were intended to. Instead, like a physical cut, these memories got stuck and became "infected"… essentially "frozen" in time, with the original images, negative beliefs, emotions, and body sensations.

Those carrying these frozen memories may be able to keep them bottled up for a while, like a dam, holding back a raging river. But without EMDR therapy, this dam will forever have a crack in it… and over time, with enough pressure, with enough stress, the compartments someone uses to hold it all together finally break… and it can all come back like raging flood. This doesn't mean that someone necessarily has one big "nervous breakdown." For many, it comes out as little floods… strong emotional reactions that occur every day, or every week.

---

[4] EMDR Institute Website, http://www.emdr.com/what-is-emdr/.

"...frozen memory is like a tiger"

To an outsider it might seem like someone's being "over-sensitive" or "overreacting." After all, the intensity of the response doesn't seem to match what's actually happening in the current situation. It may seem like they're blowing things way out of proportion. While this may be true, in truth, their response is perfectly proportional to the unhealed memories that were just triggered. They've just had old, emotional wounds ripped wide open, wounds that never fully healed right in the first place. When unhealed trauma is triggered, there is no past... as far as the survival brain is concerned, it's all happening now.

I sometimes tell my clients that a traumatically frozen memory is like a tiger, sleeping in its den. At first, it's tucked away in the darkness of its cave...

You might even pass it by and not know what's in there. Or, if you know it's in there, you might try to convince yourself it's not there by avoiding it. But the trouble with trauma is that it rarely stays asleep forever. It can be avoided, ignored, and medicated, but without EMDR therapy, you're always just one trigger away from the "tiger" waking up. And here's the thing, the situations that wake up the tiger can be everyday things, and these things actually get louder over time. They say time heals all wounds. But with posttraumatic stress, it's simply not true. Time just wakes up the tiger.

Why EMDR Therapy Works: Case Examples

To help bring to life why EMDR therapy works, in a moment I'll use a couple case examples. Please know that these are not actual clients, but rather fictional characters that represent the kinds of clients I so often see in my practice. If their names or situations resemble someone real, please know that this is purely coincidental.

Let's turn to the first example… a military veteran we'll call Bob. Bob, now in his early 40s, saw combat in Afghanistan. While he was over there, he experienced not only the pervasive sense of being on-edge and unsafe… but the intense helplessness and fear of being attacked unexpectedly and watching his buddies die in his arms.

Through no fault of his own, the intensity of these experiences overwhelmed his brain's ability to cope, and they became frozen, like that tiger in the cave… and today, every time the tiger gets poked, every time a memory wakes up, Bob re-experiences it almost as if it were happening again. His heart races, his breathing changes, his body fills with adrenaline, and he feels helpless, like he's actually going to die. The rational part of him knows that his tour of duty is over, but his brain isn't rational right now… it's in survival mode, and his body is responding accordingly.

After coming back from the war, Bob learned that a few things kept the tiger away. Becoming emotionally numb helped. The only problem is that while it helped him escape the pain, it also made him miss out on the good things in life, the things that make life worth living. Playing with his kids... enjoying the company of his wife, enjoying the beauty of nature. Numbness has a cost. He also discovered that drugs and alcohol kept the tiger from waking up. In fact, they worked pretty well! They gave him relief from the physical and emotional pain, and actually helped him feel normal for a while. But of course, we know that addiction takes its toll as well... that painful cycle of lying, hiding, shame, and isolation, that impacts the whole family. And finally, Bob could rely on his anger. Like a devoted bodyguard, his anger would spring into action any time the old, painful feelings from the past started to resurface. Anger would come to the rescue, squashing these emotions, filling him with adrenaline and power. Sure, anger could get him in trouble, but it sure felt better than being frozen in helplessness, shame, or fear.[5]

If you asked Bob about his anger, he'd tell you that he was often walking on the edge, just a moment away from not only anger, but immediate and violent rage. He learned this about himself 3 months after he got back home. He was driving to a job interview

---

[5] Howard J. Lipke, *Don't I Have a Right to be Angry?: The Heart Program for Veterans and Others Who Want to Prevent Destructive Anger* (Good Looking Software, Inc., 2013).

"... truth can't quite get from the head to the heart."

when another vehicle cut him off in traffic. Bob felt a surge of adrenaline course through his body, and an immediate desire to fight back… a deep, primal impulse to make the driver pay. With his knuckles turning white as he clutched the steering wheel, Bob tailed the perceived offender, bumper to bumper, for miles. When the light turned red, as if in a trance, he found himself getting out of his car, walking over to the vehicle, and grabbing the driver through his open window. He slammed the driver's head against his steering wheel three times before he tossed him aside and realized this big threat was actually a thin, rather small, teenage boy… probably just fresh out of driver's training.

This wasn't who Bob was, a family man who prided himself on service, sacrifice, and self-control. And yet here he was. After an arrest, court, and mandatory anger management classes, Bob was still only a moment away from doing it again. Why is this? Well, according to the AIP system understanding of the brain, Bob's behavior makes perfect sense. Actually, it's what you might expect from someone with a traumatized brain who's been through what he went through. Remember, his feelings of intense danger and helplessness from combat became frozen in his brain… his traumatic memories had been dysfunctionally stored; cut off from the adaptive information he needed to heal… Adaptive, felt truths like "I'm safe now," or "I have choices now," or "It's over."

To Bob, these truthful statements would sound nice, but without EMDR, they would never really *feel* true… they were just wishful thinking. The trouble with posttraumatic stress is that the truth can't quite get from the head to the heart. For those of you who have trouble seeing yourself in Bob, let me give you one more example that might hit closer to home. If you're married, or have been in a serious relationship, maybe this will be easier to relate to.

After a long day of work John walks through the front door, grabs a beer, and relaxes on the couch to watch tv. His wife, Sarah, had come home just a few minutes earlier, and had started washing the large pile of dishes in the sink. The minutes pass by with John, silently watching tv, and Susan, noisily scrubbing away... until finally, she breaks the silence, saying, "I thought you were going to do the dishes last night." And so it begins, another argument. As usual, it's unproductive. Tempers are raised, hurtful things are said, and it ends as he storms off and disappears to the basement. Nothing is resolved, and both John and Sarah are left feeling hurt, lonely, and misunderstood.

You don't have to be a rocket scientist to see that it's just *not* about the dishes. It rarely is. It's really about how the situation with the dishes triggered John and Susan back to their old hurts and insecurities. It's about how John not doing the dishes stirred up Susan's insecurity of not being important, and how the way Susan brought up the subject stirred up John's old insecurity of not being good enough. From an AIP perspective, the roots of these kinds of insecurities go back to old hurts, often from childhood. Even with good parents and a pretty good upbringing, no one grows up emotionally unscathed. Sticks and stones can break our bones, but words... words *can*, in fact, hurt us... planting seeds of doubt and insecurity that grow with time. The old playground saying implies that sticks and stones can truly hurt us because unlike emotional hurts, sticks and stones can inflict real bodily harm. But we now know that emotional wounds can hurt our bodies as well (*remember the ACE study?*)... Emotional wounds are just more hidden because they're located in a part of the body no one can see, the brain.

Posttraumatic stress might be easier to relate to if we could see it, like a bruise, a broken bone, or that unhealed cut we spoke of earlier. But since the wound is in the brain, it's more difficult to recognize and understand. And too many people, including many doctors, will dismiss trauma, saying "it's all in your head," or, "there's nothing physically wrong with you." If when they said this they actually meant "it's all in your head *because there's something very real happening in your brain*," that would be helpful. Unfortunately, this attitude instead conveys that someone made it all up, and maybe needs to simply toughen up and get over it. With emotional trauma, it's not that simple.

With this reality in mind, it's no surprise that couples and families often drag up the past. Events that have supposedly been forgiven resurface with a vengeance, almost as if they were happening all over again. If John and Sarah were in my office, I might ask them how things would be different if their deepest insecurities were washed away... if deep inside, John actually felt "good enough," and Susan actually felt "important."

"...even better to heal the root cause"

For many couples, this change would transform their relationship from the inside out. They'd actually be able to just argue about the dishes, and it wouldn't even be much of an argument! They'd be able to deal with what's actually in front of them, and have a proportional emotional response without being overwhelmed by a flood of past pain. If they were in my office, I would explain all this to them, and recommend that they each receive individual EMDR therapy to work through their old hurts so they can come back together and do more meaningful couples work. I would agree with them that of course, it's good to learn tools to manage their emotions. However, I'd emphasize that it's even better to heal the root cause, and that EMDR therapy could help them do that.

If you or someone you love wants freedom from those old hurts, EMDR therapy could be the ticket. But I know that doing something new can stir up anxiety, especially something like therapy. And so, to try and take all the mystery out of the process, I'll now be going over the nuts and bolts of what EMDR therapy actually looks like. I'll go through each of the Standard Protocol's 8 phases, starting with, you guessed it, Phase 1.

CHAPTER 2
HOW IT WORKS: THE 8 PHASES OF EMDR

Phase 1: History and Treatment Planning

Phase 1 of EMDR therapy, is the "Client History" Phase, which generally occurs during the first few sessions of therapy. If you decide to start EMDR therapy, you'll be asked to fill out some paperwork ahead of time, and at that first intake session with your therapist they'll try to get to know more about what brought you to therapy and what you hope to get out of it. That first session might feel more formal because of the paperwork, and because if you're using insurance, your therapist will also be needing to assess for a diagnosis… like depression, anxiety, PTSD, or whatever grouping of symptoms best explains your unique situation.

In this initial phase of EMDR, your therapist will take a thorough history and develop a treatment plan. And they'll do so with the conceptualization that the root cause of many of our problems stems from unresolved issues from the past… from unresolved traumatic memories that are cut off from that adult, truthful perspective. Your EMDR treatment plan will essentially be a list of memories in need of healing. Memories that helped shape negative views about yourself and the world around you… memories that might very well still have an emotional charge to them. Your treatment plan will include these past memories, as well as present triggers and future hypothetical situations. This is important, because EMDR is a 3 prong protocol... <u>Past</u>, <u>Present</u>, and <u>Future</u>… like 3 legs of a stool. To stay balanced, your treatment plan will help you not only heal from your past, but help you integrate this healing into your present circumstances and propel you towards a brighter and more hopeful future. With comprehensive healing, life becomes more balanced, and like that 3 legged stool, can more easily bear the heaviness of life.[6]

In taking your history, your therapist will ask questions designed to understand the links between past and present. For example, in my practice a client may come into therapy saying "I just never feel good about myself." When I hear something like this, I often ask them to reflect on that negative belief, notice where they feel it in their body, and ask them to "float

---

[6] EMDR International Association Website, https://emdria.site-ym.com/?120.

"... float back to an earlier time"

back" to an earlier time in their lives when they felt like that, maybe even as a child. Often, something will quickly come to mind, and that "something" is often a significant memory in need of reprocessing and healing.[7]

They might say something like, "I thought about when I was 16, and I came home with a B on my report card and dad asked me what was wrong with me… why didn't I get an A?" Although it might seem like things this long ago shouldn't impact us,

---

[7] EMDR International Association Website, https://emdria.site-ym.com/?120.

they often do. They're the moments where the seeds of insecurity and pain first took root in our lives, making us more sensitive to certain situations in the future. I encourage my clients not to judge their emotions or memories. Instead of beating themselves up about what they think they "should" be feeling, I encourage them to simply notice what is.[8]

This "floatback" technique I just mentioned, is one way your therapist might be looking for the origin of where your hurts and insecurities developed. And if they can find them, there's a good chance they can be healed. With clients, I often use a gardening analogy. I tell them that with trauma, regular talk therapy can be like snipping off the tops of weeds. It can help "manage" the problem, but unless you really rip it out by the roots, the problem never really goes away. One nice thing about EMDR therapy is that during this initial phase you don't have to go into great detail. Your therapist doesn't need all the details to develop their plan, just the bullet points.

At one of my trainings, I picked up the phrase, "We don't need the fine print, just the headlines." Often, this is for the best, because EMDR therapists know that talking too much about painful experiences at this stage can be a little like ripping open an old wound when we don't have the bandages ready. Before we dive into reprocessing the trauma, your therapist will try to make sure you're prepared with the

---

[8] Francine Shapiro and Deany Laliotis, *EMDR Institute Basic Training Course: Weekend 1 of the Two Part EMDR Therapy Basic Training.* Basic Training Manual (United States of America, 2017), 45.

resources you need to not only heal from your trauma, but continue to function and manage your emotions between sessions. This brings us to Phase 2.

Phase 2: Preparation

Phase 2 is "Preparation," which for many clients may only last a few sessions. Again, it all depends on how complex one's trauma is, and how able one is to cope with it. For clients with severe trauma, complex trauma, and dissociation, this phase may take longer. During this phase your therapist will assess your resources, your support system, and your ability to manage your emotions. They'll probably practice one or two self-regulation skills with you. The most common one is called either the "Safe Place" or "Calm Place" exercise. It involves visualizing a calm place in your mind, and as you do, your therapist will administer slow, bilateral stimulation... a left to right, outside distraction.[9]

The preferred method for this is the "EM" in EMDR, which stands for "eye movement." Your therapist will slowly move their hand or fingers back and forth across your field of vision. And as they do, with your head still, you'll track the movements with your eyes. As the eyes go back and forth, you simply "notice" what's happening, allowing your mind to free-associate, or naturally drift wherever it wants to go, without trying to control it. A little like daydreaming, it's not about "trying," or "performing"... it's simply about letting go... Just noticing.[10]

---

[9] EMDR International Association Website, https://emdria.site-ym.com/?1200.

[10] Francine Shapiro and Deany Laliotis, *EMDR Institute Basic Training Course: Weekend 1 of the Two Part EMDR Therapy Basic Training. Basic Training Manual* (United States of America, 2017), 31.

After a few back and forth passes of eye movements, your therapist will stop, maybe ask you to take a breath, and tell them what you noticed. At this time you simply report what you're noticing... anything at all. Any image, thought, memory, feeling, or body sensation. For example, if someone's calm place was sitting on a beach in Hawaii, after a few, slow, eye movements and a deep breath, they might say, "I noticed the warm sun on my face, and the waves gently crashing in the background... it feels good." At this point, the therapist would probably say something very simple, like "notice that," or "go with that," and proceed with more bilateral stimulation... a few more eye movements... maybe another breath... the same question... "What did you notice that time?"... an answer... "I'm feeling more relaxed now." There's more to it that this, but you get the picture.[11]

So there it is... This "Calm Place" exercise is important for a couple reasons. First, it can help you strengthen positive imagery and emotions in connection with a place that you can recall using a cue word at another time. If it works well, your therapist might encourage you to practice it outside of therapy. For example, if you're stressed out at work the next day, you can take a deep breath, say your cue word out loud, and allow your mind to drift back to that calmer state. For some, it's empowering to know that they can use a simple tool like this to change

---

[11] Francine Shapiro and Deany Laliotis, *EMDR Institute Basic Training Course: Weekend 1 of the Two Part EMDR Therapy Basic Training. Basic Training Manual* (United States of America, 2017), 43.

"... it's simply about letting go"

their thoughts and feelings fast. After learning this strategy, you'll also be able to use it as a way to calm down at the end of future therapy sessions.[12]

The second reason the "Calm Place" exercise is important is because it serves as an assessment. It will help give your therapist a better idea of how your brain processes, and how it responds to bilateral stimulation. For some, finding an "inner calm place" is very difficult, because even their calmest places are associated with pain. Again, this isn't about performing. It's not something you can pass or fail. And so it's okay if it doesn't work, because your

---

[12] Francine Shapiro and Deany Laliotis, *EMDR Institute Basic Training Course: Weekend 1 of the Two Part EMDR Therapy Basic Training. Basic Training Manual (*United States of America, 2017), 32-33.

therapist will have other strategies to help you practice emotional regulation.

For EMDR, it's good to have more than one calming strategy anyway. Like tools in the tool belt, it's nice to have options. It's nice to know that if one strategy doesn't work as well, there are other things you can try. Let's go back to our example... of someone's calm place being a beach in Hawaii, and what sometimes happens... If you recall, our hypothetical client was imagining the sensations of being on the beach, and it was calming. With each set of short eye movements, the positive feelings were enhanced. But then, during the next set of eye movements the therapist sees that calm expression on their client's face morph into a look of disgust. They ask, "What did you notice that time?" The client responds, "he's there!...my ex-husband! Now that I think of it, he wrecked that vacation... he wrecked all our vacations!"

If you end up having an experience like this, it doesn't mean that EMDR isn't working. It just means that you have pain, and your therapist will be happy to help you find another "Calm Place" you can work on together. And if it turns out that the "Calm Place" resource just isn't the right fit, as I said, there are plenty of other calming strategies your therapist can teach you. There's "Container" exercises, deep breathing, progressive muscle relaxation, guided imagery, meditation, mindfulness, prayer, and many other possibilities.[13]

During this Preparation Phase you'll also be getting to know your therapist. While they may not reveal too much about themselves personally, after a few sessions you'll get a better sense of their personality and approach. You'll have a sense about whether they know what they're doing, and if they actually care. It's a process of building trust, which is pretty important when you think about bearing your heart and soul to someone. As a therapist, I know that trust is earned over time, and I expect that my clients will at first be somewhat guarded with me. That's part of why I shared that I've done my own therapy... I get it. I may not understand what it's like to be you, but I understand what it's like to be in that vulnerable position of reaching out for support.

The beauty of EMDR is that if you feel too vulnerable, you don't have to share all the details. Remember, just the bullet points... just the headlines. And thankfully, the EMDR process is so powerful, that it tends to work even if you have your doubts about it. The bottom line with the Preparation Phase is this... your therapist just wants to make sure that before you dive into memory work you have the tools and resources you need to take care of yourself, and they'll take as long as necessary to help you get there.

---

[13] Francine Shapiro and Deany Laliotis, *EMDR Institute Basic Training Course: Weekend 1 of the Two Part EMDR Therapy Basic Training. Basic Training Manual* (United States of America, 2017), 33.

If it turns out that you don't work on memories right away, it doesn't mean that you're not doing EMDR. Remember, it's an 8 phase process, and sometimes people need to be in the Preparation Phase for a while. This is especially true if there's a history of self-harm, suicidal thoughts, or dissociation. In cases like this, moving ahead with memory work too quickly can be overwhelming, and even retraumatizing. As one trainer put it, sometimes taking it slow is the fastest way to get to the destination. Again, many clients just need a session or two of Preparation before beginning to reprocess memories. But, if it takes longer, that's okay.

Phase 3: Assessment

Phase 3 is "Assessment," which will be each time you prepare to reprocess a new men Your therapist will draw from the list of memories already written down in your EMDR treatment plan, and will choose one memory to focus on for the session. Often, they'll choose an early memory from childhood that's connected to the same negative belief that's bothering you today. This is called the "touchstone memory," and it's usually worked on first because it's where the roots of your insecurities first started to grow. If your therapist is managing their time well, they'll try to identify the memory at the very beginning of the session, or even at the previous session, keeping small talk to a minimum.

After identifying the memory, they will then begin the Assessment Phase. This involves them taking just a few minutes to ask you a series of specific questions. These questions are designed to help illicit the images, beliefs, emotions, and body sensations connected to the memory.[14]

They'll start by asking what image stands out as the worst part, and then go on to ask about what negative belief, or "Negative Cognition" about yourself goes with it. Sometimes, this deep insecurity is hard to identify, but your therapist will help you get there. Usually, the negative cognition, or "NC," will take the form of an "I statement." For example, "I'm a failure,"

---

[14] EMDR International Association Website, https://emdria.site-ym.com/?120.

ɪr "I'm not good enough," or "I'm not safe." If you have a hard time identifying your NC, your therapist might throw out a couple suggestions to see if they fit, or even show you a list of statements to choose from. For most of us, there's at least one negative belief about ourselves that's hard to shake.[15]

Identifying your core, negative cognition is so important, because it brings things into the light. It exposes the lies we picked up in childhood, and sheds light on how they distort reality. In EMDR circles, we think of negative cognitions generally falling into one of three categories... The first category is Responsibility. This could involve feeling defective, like "I'm not good enough," or "I'm a disappointment." Or, it could involve action, like "I should have done something," or "I'm weak." The second category is Safety/Vulnerability. This category involves beliefs like "I'm not safe," or "I can't trust anyone." And the third category is Power/Control, which involves statements like "I'm out of control," or "I can't handle it." Thankfully, you don't have to remember all this, because your therapist will keep it all in mind and help you get there.[16]

Once your negative cognition is identified, your therapist will ask about what positive statement you'd prefer to believe about yourself instead. Often, this

[15] Francine Shapiro and Deany Laliotis, *EMDR Institute Basic Training Course: Weekend 1 of the Two Part EMDR Therapy Basic Training. Basic Training Manual* (United States of America, 2017) 48-54.

[16] Francine Shapiro and Deany Laliotis, *EMDR Institute Basic Training Course: Weekend 1 of the Two Part EMDR Therapy Basic Training. Basic Training Manual* (United States of America, 2017), 50-52.

positive statement will be the opposite of the negative cognition. For example, someone who grew up thinking "I'm not good enough," generally wants to believe the words "I am good enough." Someone whose negative belief is "I'm not safe," generally wants to believe "I'm safe now," or, "it's over." After identifying this positive cognition, your therapist will ask you how true the positive statement feels on a 1 to 7 Validity of Cognition (VOC) scale. They'll use this VOC scale to establish a baseline for how true the truth actually <u>feels</u> when connected to the memory. At a later time during reprocessing, as the memory becomes calm, they'll return to this scale to see if these positive words still fit, or if there's been a change.[17]

After assessing how true your positive belief feels, your therapist will then instruct you to bring up the memory and the negative words, and tell them what emotions you feel "now." After describing what you feel, they'll go on ask how disturbing the memory feels on a 0-10 Subjective Units of Disturbance (SUD) scale, where 0 is calm and 10 is the worst. Finally, they'll ask you where you feel the distress in your body. This concludes the Assessment Phase. While it might seem like a lengthy step-by-step process, in practice, this part of the protocol actually flows pretty smoothly, and in my experience, once the negative cognition is properly identified, the process goes

---

[17] Francine Shapiro and Deany Laliotis, *EMDR Institute Basic Training Course: Weekend 1 of the Two Part EMDR Therapy Basic Training. Basic Training Manual* (United States of America, 2017), 53-54

rather quickly. Again, the goal isn't to get into talk therapy here, but to stay connected to the traumatically-stored memory network and actually light it up. An EMDR trainer once pointed out that like a house with many sides, the Assessment Phase of EMDR helps us come at the memory from several angles. The picture, negative cognition, emotions, and body sensations are all ways to purposely light up the painful memory; not to be cruel, but to activate the memory networks that desperately need to be healed. [18]

Lighting up the most wounded parts of the past can be difficult, and I often talk with my clients about how in our daily lives it's normal to try and avoid these uncomfortable emotions and memories... I know I do. But I also encourage them with the idea that if they're willing to commit to the EMDR healing process, they only need to face these things head on for about one hour a week... just one hour to face the things they'd rather avoid. Like a good workout, it can be exhausting, but it's worth it. And thankfully, your therapist won't just open up the can of worms and leave you hanging. They understand that when it comes to trauma, talk therapy alone doesn't necessarily lead to healing. The Assessment Phase isn't an end in itself, but rather the build up to where much of the healing takes place... The Desensitization Phase.

---

[18] Francine Shapiro and Deany Laliotis, *EMDR Institute Basic Training Course: Weekend 1 of the Two Part EMDR Therapy Basic Training. Basic Training Manual* (United States of America, 2017), 53-54.

"... lighting up the most wounded parts of the past"

Phase 4: Desensitization

Phase 4 is "Desensitization," which focuses on using bilateral stimulation to reprocess a traumatic memory. Again, the preferred method of bilateral stimulation is eye movements. However, alternating buzzers held in your hands, audio tones heard through headphones, or even physical taps on your hands or knees, are also common, effective methods. Sometimes, for whatever reason, eye movements don't work as well as they could. Usually it works... but when it doesn't, sometimes reasons like dry eyes, eye soreness, dizziness, or difficulty focusing are involved.

However, even in cases where it at first seems like it's not working, your therapist can change the speed, direction, and duration of the eye movements, and sometimes this is enough to break through the barrier and get things moving. If not, using buzzers, taps, or tones serves as a wonderful back-up. If using eye movements, your therapist will sit in front of you and to the side, as our basic training puts it, "like two ships passing." The therapist's hand movements will be a few feet in front of your face... enough space so you don't feel crowded, but not so far away that you can't focus.

Your therapist will also share some basic instructions around what to expect during this phase of EMDR. They'll remind you that after each set of bilateral stimulation, they'll ask for specific feedback, emphasizing that whatever comes up is okay, and that sometimes things might change, and sometimes they might not. Rather than judging your experience, you'll be encouraged to simply "let go" and see what comes to mind. They might even share the common metaphor of EMDR being like riding on a train or bus, looking out the window, and just "watching the scenery go by." While the bilateral passes are happening, you'll be free associating. You won't be talking, only noticing… observing the thoughts, feelings, images, or memories that come to mind. I sometimes tell my clients that it's like pushing play on a movie you've never seen before. You don't have to direct the movie… you just have to sit back and see what happens. Finally, your therapist should remind you that you can always put up your hand as a "stop signal," a reminder that you can stop anytime to take a break if you need to.[19]

At the end of the Assessment Phase, where the therapist asks all those strategic questions to light up the traumatic memory network, they'll then pull it all together by summarizing your answers, asking you to think about the image, the negative belief, the emotions, and where you feel it in your body, and then ask you to follow their fingers as they begin the

---

[19] Francine Shapiro and Deany Laliotis, *EMDR Institute Basic Training Course: Weekend 1 of the Two Part EMDR Therapy Basic Training. Basic Training Manual* (United States of America, 2017), 55-56.

"... Just notice"

first set of eye movements. Once the eye movements start, as a therapist I usually don't say much. Occasionally, I might say something just to reassure the client I'm with them, saying something like, "Just notice," reminding them that there are no "supposed to's," and to just "let whatever happens, happen."[20]

Once your therapist starts bilateral stimulation, they may start with about 30 seconds of back and forth passes for the first set, but may go longer or shorter, catering to your unique situation. They'll be paying close attention to your breathing, skin coloration, and other non-verbals including your facial expression and posture. Depending on what they see,

[20] Francine Shapiro and Deany Laliotis, *EMDR Institute Basic Training Course: Weekend 1 of the Two Part EMDR Therapy Basic Training. Basic Training Manual* (United States of America, 2017), 55-56.

they may change the speed or direction of the eye movements, as sometimes these subtle changes can help with reprocessing. When concluding a set, they'll bring the bilateral stimulation to a stop, and say something like, "Let it go, and take a breath." After pausing, they'll then ask you what you noticed. You'll then briefly share what was happening, and your therapist will begin another set of bilateral, saying something like "Go with that," or "notice that."[21]

During this Desensitization Phase it's normal to have emotions intensify, because we're digging up old memories that have sometimes been buried for a long time… and again, just because it happened a long time ago doesn't mean that "time has healed all wounds." While this holds true for many memories, traumatic memories are stored differently in our brains. And so when they're opened up, people are sometimes surprised to find how emotionally raw they actually are… surprised to find that some of the original sights, sounds, emotions, body sensations, and beliefs resurface as fresh as if it were happening for the first time.

Thankfully, the bilateral stimulation, or "BLS," combined with the brain's natural capacity to heal, begins to desensitize these over-sensitive emotions, and after a few sets of eye movements, often the body will begin to calm down. Amazingly, while the

---

[21] Francine Shapiro and Deany Laliotis, *EMDR Institute Basic Training Course: Weekend 1 of the Two Part EMDR Therapy Basic Training. Basic Training Manual* (United States of America, 2017), 55-56.

"... the tiger is becoming sleepier, smaller, and far less scary"

body's calming down, at the very same time, positive, adaptive information starts linking into the old memory, reshaping it from a more truthful perspective. It's almost like an old wound that never healed finally gets cleaned out, stitched up, and bandaged for the first time. Or to go back to my earlier metaphor, it's like we woke up the tiger on purpose, but then discover that the tiger is becoming sleepier, smaller, and far less scary than we thought.

After each set of eye movements, a breath, and a brief report about what you noticed, as long as things continue to change, your therapist will continue to say something like, "notice that," or "go with that," or "see what happens next" before beginning another set of eye movements. If processing veers off in a direction not related to the target memory or if things stop changing, they'll then go back to "target," saying something like, "When you go back to where you started… back to the original memory you began with today… what are you noticing now?" This can be enough to get things moving again, and can help your therapist understand if there's been any changes in how you're storing the memory.[22]

And sometimes, you might feel stuck. For whatever reason, the memory isn't changing… the adaptive information needed to heal just isn't linking in naturally. In these cases, your therapist might use a Cognitive Interweave, which is simply a gentle nudge from the outside to help get things moving again. It might be gently reminding you of something, or asking a question. Each situation is different, so the the interweave will be catered to your unique memory network and belief system. Often, a good interweave can get things going again and help you move the memory to resolution. When things stop changing, they'll once again go back to target and check on the

[22] Francine Shapiro and Deany Laliotis, *EMDR Institute Basic Training Course: Weekend 1 of the Two Part EMDR Therapy Basic Training. Basic Training Manual* (United States of America, 2017), 57.

original memory. And when the memory's healed you'll be able to feel it.[23]

You may be surprised, because the emotional intensity is no longer part of the memory. When a memory has healed, my clients will say things like, "I know it happened, but now it's like I'm watching it from a distance instead of being in it." Others will say the memory feels "foggy," or "hard to even connect to." Still others will report it's like "watching it on a TV screen," with a sense of distance and perspective. They still know what happened, but their sensory experience of the memory has changed.

Often, this new sense of calm will be accompanied by new insights, helpful associations, and a positive truth statement that finally feels true… typically a version of the Positive Cognition we identified earlier in the Assessment Phase (Phase 3). I tell clients that we can know a memory is really healed when you can think about the worst part of it, feel completely calm in your body, and actually have the truth about yourself feel true. Emphasis here is on the feel… truth that can be felt in the gut, or the heart. And remarkably, for many clients, a day, a week, a month, or even years later, the change has lasted.

With EMDR, the changes are lasting because the memories have truly been reprocessed, allowing the client's AIP system, (remember, that adaptive information processing system we all have?), to heal

---

[23] Francine Shapiro and Deany Laliotis, *EMDR Institute Basic Training Course: Weekend 2 of the Two Part EMDR Therapy Basic Training. Basic Training Manual* (United States of America, 2017), 47-59.

naturally. Like a smartphone getting an update, bugs are fixed, and the whole system now runs smoother. The results are remarkable… memories are actually stored differently in the brain. During an EMDR session, if your therapist asks you to go back to the original memory, they may ask you to give them a new reading on the 0-10 SUD scale, where 0 is calm, or neutral, and 10 is the worst you can imagine. When you report that it's down to a 0, and it stays there, it's then time for the Installation Phase.

Phase 5: Installation

Phase 5 is "Installation," which seamlessly follows the Desensitization Phase. When the SUD scale is at a 0, your therapist knows that the Desensitization Phase is over and that it's time to ask you if the original positive words you came up with still fit, or if there's another statement that fits better. After you settle on the positive self-statement that fits now, they'll ask you to think about the original experience and those positive words, and then again measure how true the statement feels now from 1-7, with 1, being completely false, all the way up to 7, being completely true. They will likely follow your answer with another set of BLS. Sometimes, this draws out more traumatic material that needs to heal, but often, at this point, the negative stuff has been mostly cleared away, and the positive thoughts and feelings are being reinforced and strengthened. Once the belief gets to a solid 7 on the VOC scale and stays there, we know it's time to move on to the Body Scan.
[24]

---

[24] Francine Shapiro and Deany Laliotis, *EMDR Institute Basic Training Course: Weekend 1 of the Two Part EMDR Therapy Basic Training. Basic Training Manual* (United States of America, 2017), 64-65.

Phase 6: Body Scan

Phase 6 is the "Body Scan." The Body Scan is important because sometimes our brains hold onto a piece of a painful memory, and even when it feels like it's all been dealt with, a small feeling in the body might indicate that there's more to heal. A subtle headache, tension in the neck, or a small uneasiness in the stomach... all examples indicating that there might be more traumatic material in the memory network that needs to be reprocessed. The Body Scan's important, because it recognizes the mind-body connection, and how painful memories can be experienced in the body. To do the Body Scan, your therapist will ask you to do the following according to the EMDR standard protocol...

"Close your eyes, holding in mind the original experience and the words (I then repeat their positive cognition). Then bring your attention to the different parts of your body, starting with your head and working downward. Any place you notice any unusual sensation, tell me." If there's tension left, they'll use more bilateral stimulation to help you reprocess whatever's left. And if your body feels calm, they'll probably use BLS to help strengthen and solidify the feelings of calm and any other positive sensations in the body. As with installation, sometimes BLS can reveal more trauma that needs to be reprocessed. When the body scan is finally clear, meaning that your body feels completely calm, then it's time to move on to the Closure Phase.[25]

[25] Francine Shapiro and Deany Laliotis, *EMDR Institute Basic Training Course: Weekend 1 of the Two Part EMDR Therapy Basic Training. Basic Training Manual* (United States of America, 2017), 66-67.

Phase 7: Closure

Phase 7 is "Closure." Remember how back in the Preparation Phase I talked about resources like the "Calm Place" exercise? Well, this is a good time to use it. Your therapist should reserve at least 5 minutes, sometimes more, at the end of a session to help you shift gears back to the real world. They may ask you to use your Calm Place, Container, or another calming technique, and since you've practiced it before, your body will already be trained to respond… because it will have already been conditioned to shift emotional states. This will hopefully help you leave the office in a calm state, ready to face your day.

Your therapist may remind you of what to expect between sessions, and to record your experiences in a log or journal. They'll let you know that even though the therapy session is ending, your brain will continue to process after you leave. Sometimes this leads to thoughts, feelings, insights or dreams that are related to what you worked on. And if any of these responses are distressing, you can always use your calming strategies at home."[26] I also remind my clients that if things come up, they can keep that same mindful stance of "just noticing," without feeling like they have to solve everything between sessions. However, I affirm that if there are

---

[26] Francine Shapiro and Deany Laliotis, *EMDR Institute Basic Training Course: Weekend 1 of the Two Part EMDR Therapy Basic Training. Basic Training Manual* (United States of America, 2017), 68-69.

other things like journaling, talking, or doing art, etc., that helps them work through their emotions, that's okay too. The important thing is that they stay safe, feel supported, and can take care of themselves between now and the next session.

Phase 8: Reevaluation

Phase 8 is "Reevaluation." This Phase occurs at the beginning of the next therapy appointment, as a follow-up after every reprocessing session. It's a way for your therapist to check up on what you processed the previous week, and figure out where to go from there. If the memory that was worked on at the last session was completed, it may still be calm. If so, you can then check that one off the list, and shift focus to the next memory on the treatment plan. Occasionally, a memory that was calm the week before will now have some distress attached to it. If so, this just means that there's something else about the memory that needs healing, and it's good that it came out! Because if it didn't, it could cause problems down the road. So, even unexpected negative emotions can be seen as an opportunity to have the most thorough healing possible.

It's very common to reevaluate a memory that wasn't completed at the last session. Working through these memories can be like peeling an onion, and sometimes we just can't get through all the layers of a memory in one session. If the previous memory wasn't completed, then after a very brief discussion of what EMDR-related thoughts or feelings came up during the week, your therapist will help you pick up where you left off from the last session. To get things going, they'll use an abbreviated version of the Assessment Phase, asking the same questions as before to help you connect to the memory network. But this time, they'll omit questions related to what you believe about the memory, as these cognitions have already been established. As before, they'll ask you to notice it all, and follow their fingers. You're then "off the races," working through more traumatic material, essentially dipping back into the previous phases until the memory is desensitized to a 0, the truth feels like a solid 7, and the body scan is clear.[27]

---

[27] Francine Shapiro and Deany Laliotis, *EMDR Institute Basic Training Course: Weekend 1 of the Two Part EMDR Therapy Basic Training. Basic Training Manual* (United States of America, 2017), 80.

Three Prong Protocol

Well, there you have it. The EMDR, 8-Phase, Standard Protocol. A couple things to note about these phases. Sometimes people are confused about how they fit together, because they don't always seem to go in order. So, to clarify, Phases 1 and 2, (Client History and Preparation), only happen once. Although an EMDR therapist might occasionally dip back into these phases to gather more information or firm up some resources, these two earliest phases tend to be over once a client is ready to start reprocessing memories.

Unlike Phases 1 and 2, Phases 3 through 8 can happen for every memory that's worked on... that's because each memory needs to be assessed (Phase 3) and desensitized (Phase 4), the positive cognition needs to be installed (Phase 5), the body scan needs to be completed (Phase 6), the session needs to close (Phase 7), and the memory needs to be checked on at the following session (Phase 8). So, if EMDR is going well, it's not uncommon to go from Phase 3 all the way through Phase 7 in a single session.

I like to remind my clients that not only is it a 8-Phase protocol, but it's also a 3 prong protocol, focusing on not only the past, but also the present and the future. Remember the 3-legged stool? it takes a past, present, and future approach to support a comprehensive healing process. Phases 3-8 will be followed for each memory on the treatment plan until all past memories are processed. At this point, present triggers and future situations are addressed. Present triggers are situations that cause problems in your everyday life, and are processed in the same way as past memories. And for every present trigger, there's also a related future template. The future template is basically a shortlist of hypothetical future scenarios related to this present trigger.

The goal… to take the same calm, strength, and positive felt truth into the future with confidence. To be able to rehearse these future situations in your mind like a movie, working through any emotional barriers along the way. When any stress pops up, your therapist will help you process through it with BLS, and when positive stuff links in, they'll use BLS to strengthen it. When this step is completed… when you can get through the whole movie without distress, well… then it's time to celebrate! At this point, not only have you had the guts to face some truly hard things, but you've come out on the other side with a transformed mind. Deeper calm, more peace, more confidence, and a more truthful perspective on who you really are.

Now that we're through the nuts and bolts of EMDR, the remainder of our time together will be going over common questions people have about EMDR. Here we go… Question 1…. Does EMDR therapy actually work?

CHAPTER 3
QUESTIONS AND ANSWERS

Does EMDR Therapy Actually Work?

In short, the answer is absolutely, yes! It actually works! I've seen it work for hundreds of my own clients, and my experience is shared firsthand by tens of thousands of therapists and millions of clients worldwide. Its power and effectiveness is also backed up by the numbers. According to the EMDR Institute, at the time of this course, "More than 30 positive controlled studies have been done on EMDR. Some of the studies show that 84%-90% of single-trauma victims no longer have post-traumatic stress disorder after only"… that's right, only "three 90-minute sessions."[28]

"Another study, funded by the HMO Kaiser Permanente, found that 100% of the single incident trauma victims and 77% of multiple trauma victims no longer were diagnosed with PTSD after only six

---

[28] EMDR Institute Website, http://www.emdr.com/what-is-emdr/.

50-minute sessions. In another study, 77% of combat veterans were free of PTSD in 12 sessions." As I mentioned earlier, "There has been so much research on EMDR that it is now recognized as an effective form of treatment for trauma and other disturbing experiences by organizations such as the American Psychiatric Association, the World Health Organization and the Department of Defense."[29]

Given its success with treating the most traumatic memories for those with PTSD, it's no surprise that it's also helped people struggling with a wide variety of other common issues that bring people to therapy. According the the EMDRIA website (again, that's the EMDR International Association), clinicians have reported success using EMDR in treatment of panic attacks, complicated grief, disturbing memories, phobias, pain disorders, performance anxiety, stress reduction, addictions, sexual and/or physical abuse, body dysmorphic disorders, and personality disorders. [30] As we speak, EMDR is helping people around the world to heal not only from intense trauma, but also from the everyday hurts, fears, and insecurities that bring so many of us to counseling.

After being trained in EMDR therapy, my counseling practice changed forever. Situations where clients normally would have been in therapy for years, were now finding resolution within weeks or

---

[29] EMDR Institute Website, http://www.emdr.com/what-is-emdr/.
[30] EMDR International Association Website, emdria.org.

"... therapy is an act of courage"

months. I started to see people actually heal in a way that was efficient, genuine, and lasting. While EMDR does tend to work faster than other therapies, I don't want you to come away with the idea that it's a quick fix. Despite its healing power, sometimes it can still take longer than people expect. And in these cases, it doesn't mean that someone's doing something wrong. It just means that everyone's healing process is different. Just being in therapy is an act of courage, and for this reason alone, anyone going through EMDR therapy has a lot to be proud of. Not everyone has the guts to face this stuff.

In my years as an EMDR therapist I've had the privilege of walking with so many courageous clients, and it's a joy to think that I had a role in their healing process. I've seen firsthand how after EMDR therapy, someone who was abused or neglected as a child can think about the worst of it and feel a sense of calm inside. They can finally say, "I was just a kid, and it's not my fault," and actually believe it. After EMDR therapy, the military veteran, assault victim, or accident survivor can feel the same sense of peace and perspective. They can finally say and actually believe, "I'm safe now," "It's over," or "I did the best I could."

So, I've now given you all the details on EMDR. I've described each of its 8 phases, talked about its 3-prong approach, and explained the AIP system that helps our brains to heal. I've also described the 8 phases in detail, helping you see what the process actually looks like. And in our time together, I've also had the privilege of sharing a lot with you from my personal experience with EMDR. However, even if you take me out of the equation, the research speaks for itself. So, you might be thinking… "Do I need EMDR?" Or, "does my spouse, or family member, or child need EMDR?"

My short answer is "Yes, we could probably all benefit from therapy, and EMDR is the most effective and powerful therapy I know." But I'll be the first to admit that I'm biased. I don't see therapy as something you do after things have started falling apart… although, it's definitely a good idea to get

"... live life to the fullest."

therapy if this is happening. I view therapy as an opportunity to become the best person you can be and live life to the fullest. In that sense, I see it as something we can do proactively, rather than reactively. Of course, only your therapist can truly determine when you're ready to reprocess traumatic memories. So, this brings us to another common question... "How do I find a good EMDR Therapist?"

How do I Find a Good EMDR Therapist

If you've never done therapy before, getting started can feel a little overwhelming. Thankfully, there are some good websites out there. There are two, in particular, that come to mind. First, EMDR.com. EMDR.com is the website for the EMDR Institute, the organization founded by Francine Shapiro herself. Here you can find a directory of all the therapists who have been trained by her staff.

Another helpful website is EMDRIA.org, which is the official website for the EMDR International Association. I prefer this directory, because you can search not only by geographic location, but also by experience level. If you browse this site, you'll see that while all the therapists have completed an EMDR therapy basic training and are qualified to provide the therapy, some therapists have actually went on to receive an additional certification by EMDRIA. While not always the case, choosing an EMDRIA certified therapist does increase the likelihood of getting a good EMDR therapist. If your therapist is EMDRIA certified, it likely means that they have a strong interest in EMDR therapy, and have invested significant time and resources in order to obtain this status.

In addition to completing mandatory continuing education specifically in EMDR therapy, these therapists have also paid for an additional 20 hours of consultation with an EMDRIA Approved Consultant.

During these 20 consultation hours, they talked through clinical situations, received critical feedback, and were challenged to demonstrate mastery of the Basic EMDR Protocol. Finally, although far fewer in number, the EMDRIA therapist directory also lists EMDRIA Approved Consultants... The ones who are not only certified, but who also provide the consultation so other therapists can get certified. These Approved Consultants have received another 20 hours of consultation, specifically on how they guide other EMDR therapists.

A good question to ask any EMDR therapist you're considering, is whether or not they received their training from trainer approved by the EMDR International Association. I say this because there are a few courses floating around out there that aren't EMDRIA approved. They're inexpensive and very brief, and don't give a therapist the knowledge or practice they need to be good at it. However, if the therapist got their training from the EMDR Institute, EMDR-HAP (that's the EMDR Humanitarian Assistance Programs / Trauma Recovery), or any other EMDRIA approved training, you're good to go.

When clients seek me out for EMDR therapy, sometimes they've found me on EMDR.com, or EMDRIA.org. But honestly, most of them have heard about me through word of mouth or because they did a google search, read my bio, and found something

"... stick it out for at least a few sessions."

about my profile that stood out to them… something that drew them to me versus the other therapists in their area. If you're searching for an EMDR therapist, I would definitely recommend reading the bios of the therapists you're considering. This will help you get a better sense of who they are, and if their personality will be a good fit or not. And if you're still not sure, chatting with a prospective therapist for a few minutes on the phone can sometimes provide the clarity you need. Although it's not common, it's certainly something you can insist on when you make that first phone call.

I remind people that there are niches even within the EMDR community. While any EMDR therapist can treat PTSD, some also specialize in addiction, or eating disorders, or complex trauma, or dissociation… the list could go on and on. If you have a particular niche or subspecialty that's important to you, sometimes, there's no substitute for a good Google search. Simply type in "EMDR therapist" and whatever keywords you think are relevant, and start clicking through the results. Chances are, you'll find a good number of therapist close by, many of whom may not be a member of EMDRIA. EMDRIA has a few thousand members, but there are tens of thousands of trained EMDR therapist out there.

Often, the best ones have built a successful career specializing in EMDR therapy, and will wear it on their sleeve. They'll make their use of EMDR prominent in their bio because they realize it's not just one tool in a bag of tricks… it's a whole way of approaching therapy and understanding how healing happens. Finally, after you've picked a therapist, I usually encourage people to stick it out for at least a few sessions because it will probably take at least a few sessions for your therapist to get a good history and get through the Preparation Phase. However, if at any point you realize that the therapist just isn't a good fit, it's okay to quit and find a new one. If EMDR doesn't work, it's probably not because of EMDR, it's probably because the therapist wasn't using it properly. Alright, so let's say you've decided on your therapist and have your first session on the calendar. One question that still comes up is, "How long is an EMDR session?"

How Long is an EMDR Therapy Session?

In an ideal world, EMDR sessions would all be 90 minutes long. In the Client History and Preparation Phases, EMDR therapy looks very similar to other therapies. Your therapist will ask you thoughtful questions, get to know your history, and try to understand your present concerns. As mentioned earlier, like a good detective, they'll be paying close attention to any experiences, or memories that may have shaped the way you see yourself or the world around you.

I say the sessions should be 90 minutes long, because this is the recommended standard of care. A longer session like this becomes especially helpful when reprocessing memories during the Desensitization Phase. This is because for most EMDR therapy sessions, it takes some time to reevaluate the memory from the session before, and it takes some time to wind down at the end. Having a longer session helps ensure that the chunk of time in the middle is long enough to really work through the trauma. In my experience, having a full, 90 minutes helps the session not to feel rushed.

Unfortunately, we don't live in an ideal world, and most EMDR sessions are 45-55 minutes long. The reason, like it or not, is insurance companies. While most insurances have finally warmed up to EMDR therapy and acknowledged its legitimacy, they will rarely pay for more than an hour session. Since most people can't afford to pay for extra therapy time out of pocket, they're left with what insurance will cover. So, if you have the money to spend I would recommend requesting longer EMDR sessions. You'll have more time, cover more ground, and may even finish your course of therapy faster. However, if you're like most people and need to stay within your insurance network, you can expect to have sessions that last just under an hour.

If your therapist says they only have 45-minute appointments available, you may want to insist on finding an appointment time closer to 55 minutes if your insurance will cover it. Typically, they leave it up to the therapist to bill for either length of time, depending on what they feel is necessary. It may not seem like much of a difference, but every minute counts when you're trying to have a quality EMDR experience. In my personal opinion, an experienced EMDR therapist can probably still help you with a shorter session if they manage the time really well. However, it's not ideal. In most situations, you really do need the full 55 minutes in order to have enough time to begin the session properly, adequately process the memory, and then wind down and leave the session feeling calm. So, hopefully that helps answer the question about the length of any single EMDR session. The next common question is related… "How long does the Entire EMDR Therapy Process Take?"

How Long Does the Entire Therapy Process Take?

When I talk with prospective clients interested in EMDR therapy, this question comes up quite a bit… and it's a great question. It helps to know how much time, energy, and money you'll be investing in something, especially something as important as therapy. But unfortunately, there isn't a clear cut answer on this, because everyone's situation is different. I tell my clients that I'll be able to better answer their question as I get to know their story and better understand what they've been through. However, I sometimes say I think it's a good idea for them to commit to at least ten sessions. I say this because I want to be thorough, and because I know that while EMDR works faster than most therapies, it still takes time.

For healing to be thorough, it needs enough time to flow through all 8 phases, and address the past, the present, and the future. So, if you start EMDR and your therapist takes things a little slower, it's possible they're not being focused in their approach. However, it's more likely that they're simply pacing the process according to your unique situation. If the process seems to be going slow, then you can always ask them about it. In all likelihood, it doesn't mean that something's wrong. It just means that for it to be safe and effective, your therapist is taking things one step at a time. Remember, even if everything falls into place and your coping skills are strong, you still probably won't begin reprocessing memories until the third or fourth session.

How long EMDR takes for you will depend on not only how strong your coping skills are, but also on how many layers of trauma you've experienced in life. If you've had a single incident trauma, like an accident, an assault, or some other one-time event, research suggests that you may find considerable relief within just a handful of sessions. If you're trauma is more complex, it will probably take longer.

In my practice, I often see clients for EMDR therapy between 3 and 6 months. For clients who have more complex trauma and dissociation, the process may last several years. For example, if a child experiences something so horrific or disturbing that their normal coping systems are overwhelmed, they may develop a dissociative disorder... that is, the ability to repress memories, and disconnect from certain parts of their personality to emotionally survive. Often, this involves certain emotional parts of the self holding onto the traumatic memories, while the other, more apparently normal parts of self are completely shielded from these memories, unable to remember them, feel them, or even know they exist. For severely traumatized or neglected children, developing the ability to dissociate can be lifesaving.

Some of you may have heard stories about the heart-breaking conditions within so many orphanages

"... our brains do what they have to do to survive."

in Eastern Europe. While the children were diapered and fed, many were deprived of play, exploration, and physical touch. The result... young children, silently staring off into space with lifeless eyes... They had all stopped crying, because they already learned long ago that it didn't work... no one came to help. When we're in danger, we often try to fight... and if we can't fight, we try to run away... and if we can't run away... well, then we freeze, submit, shut-down, or collapse, and basically prepare to die. The bottom line, our brains do what they have to do to survive. But the coping skills that help us survive childhood are often not as effective in adulthood.

I could say a lot more about complex trauma and dissociation, but we'll have to save that for another day. The reason I bring all this up is to show how different everyone's story is. EMDR therapy for someone with a relatively "healthy" childhood who was in a traumatic car accident, might look very different than EMDR therapy with someone who as a child, grew up being physically and sexually abused for years on end. All this being said, your EMDR therapist may not be able to tell you exactly how long therapy will last, because everyone's story is different.

However, as your therapist gets to know you better, and time passes, things may become more clear. As they identify memory targets, present triggers, and future templates, and then begin reprocessing work with bilateral stimulation, they'll have a much better sense for how long it might take. In my practice I make a point of periodically reviewing the EMDR treatment plan with my clients in order to discuss progress on goals and our plan moving forward. My encouragement to you would be to find a therapist you trust, and if, as the process unfolds, you feel like it's helping, just hang in there and keep the conversation going. So, now that we've taken a look at how long EMDR therapy lasts, let's turn to money. "How much does EMDR therapy cost?"

How Much Does EMDR Therapy Cost?

Put simply, EMDR costs about the same as any other legitimate model of therapy, and your out of pocket cost will largely depend on whether or not you're using health insurance. If you're paying cash, you should expect to pay somewhere between $100 and $200 a session. If your therapist is not yet fully licensed, or if you're receiving care from a non-profit mental health clinic, you may be able to keep the costs down. Unlicensed therapists generally charge less because they're less experienced, and non-profits often can charge less because they have multiple revenue streams, can do fundraising, and, as the name "non-profit" suggests, measure success in ways that aren't tied to the "bottom line." There's also a chance that you might find a licensed therapist willing to reduce their rates on a sliding fee scale, and you might qualify for this lower rate if you're experiencing financial hardship.

In my practice, I currently charge $220 an hour. This rate is a reflection of many factors including not only my skill, education, and experience, but also the rates of other therapists in the area. However, even though this is my rate, most of my clients never pay this much because I accept their health insurance. This is an important point... when you're therapist shopping, don't be scared away by their rate if they're "in-network" with your health insurance. Because here's what happens... When I submit my rate to a client's insurance company, they don't typically reimburse me at my rate, they instead reimburse me what is sometimes called the "allowable amount." This is the amount they agreed to pay me in the contract I signed with them. And the difference between my rate and what they actually pay is written off... it's forgiven. Unless... unless you're out of network. If you're out of network, then you may get stuck with the full rate.

All this isn't unique to EMDR. The costs for receiving EMDR therapy are generally the same as for any other therapy. For insurance companies to pay, they only need a diagnosis, and a code indicating the length of each session... all information your therapist provides to them as part of their standard billing routine. With rare exceptions, most insurance companies won't even know what kind of therapy you're receiving. As long as they're being billed by a therapist or organization that they're contracted with, it's not really an issue. So, barring an audit of records by the insurance company or an authorization request for more sessions to be covered, the question shifts away from "how much does EMDR cost," and back to the broader question, "how much does therapy cost in general?"

The only surefire way to know for sure whether or not therapy will be covered is to do the following... after identifying the EMDR therapist you'd like to see,

"... think about the cost of <u>not</u> doing therapy."

get out your insurance card, and call the customer service number on the back. Follow the prompts to talk with a customer service representative about your benefits, and ask them what your benefits are for in-network versus out of network providers of mental health visits in an office setting. They should be able to tell you how much, if any, is covered, including any deductible, copays, or coinsurance that you might be obligated to pay out of pocket.

If you aren't familiar with these terms, your health insurance deductible is the amount you need to pay up front <u>before</u> the insurance will kick in and start paying. Depending on your plan, your deductible could be $0.00, $500.00, or all the way up to $10,000. It just depends on your plan. Some plans will also have co-pays, a set payment you'd have to pay at each session. Often, a co-pay will be a smaller amount, like $20 or $30 a session. Finally, coinsurance is similar to a co-pay, but rather than being a set dollar amount, it's a certain percentage of the cost of services. For example, if your co-pay was 30%, you would be responsible for paying $30.00 for a $100.00 session after your deductible has been met.

When money is a barrier to receiving EMDR therapy, I encourage people to think about the cost of not doing therapy. I encourage them to think of it as an investment in their happiness and in their future. However, many of us just don't have this mentality. So, to challenge our thinking patterns for a moment, why is it, that when the "Check Engine" light pops up on the dashboard of our vehicle we don't just ignore it?

Well, unfortunately, some of us do ignore it because the time and money it takes to go the mechanic isn't fun. However, for most of us that little light wears us down. We eventually bring in the vehicle to get checked because we know that if we ignore it too long it can come back to bite us. What could have been fixed for a few hundred dollars now has become a major problem that costs us

"... something needs attention under the hood."

thousands. To not do routine maintenance of our vehicles just costs us more in the long run.

It's the same with our mental and physical health. Our stress level, our broken relationships, our over-sensitive emotional responses... they're all "Check Engine" lights popping up, screaming that something needs attention under the hood. Something needs healing. Something has to change. And because our minds and bodies are so connected, ignoring these warning signs is just kicking the problem down the road. Just like neglecting our vehicles, neglecting our bodies and minds will catch up with us. In light of all this, I encourage people to see therapy not as a cost, but as an investment... an investment in themselves that could pay dividends for years to come.

If the money just simply isn't there, I advise people that they might consider coming every other week instead of every week. This alone would cut the cost of therapy in half. Also, I sometimes brainstorm with them to see if there's anyone in their life that would be willing to support them and invest in them... someone who cares about their mental health and would be willing to shoulder some of the financial burden. At the end of the day, the question is not only "Can I afford to do EMDR therapy?," but, "Can I afford not to do EMDR therapy?" The last common question I get is, "How do I Know if I Need EMDR Therapy?"

How do I Know if I Need EMDR Therapy?

Often, people know about EMDR because they've heard that it can cure PTSD. People will say things like "Well, I've never been to war or anything… I don't think I would qualify." When this comes up, I validate that we all have our private wars… they may not be on the battlefield, but the pain is still real. And the trauma is still real. Remember back to the AIP model? Any time our brain becomes overwhelmed by an intense experience, memories tend to become dysfunctionally stored… like that cut that won't heal naturally because it became infected.

You can have posttraumatic stress without officially meeting the diagnostic criteria for PTSD. And while it's true that EMDR is famous for treating PTSD, it can help for a wide range of issues. It's such a powerful therapeutic approach because it recognizes the impact of trauma in our lives, and provides a clear, research-proven method for healing this trauma. So, even if you don't have PTSD, there's a very good chance you still have trauma in your past. And if you have trauma in your past, there's a good chance it's affecting your life… possibly holding you back more than you think. So right now, I'd like to go through three specific warning signs to keep an eye out for, because they might indicate you're dealing with unhealed trauma. Each one of them is a form of avoidance, a way to escape the pain. They are… minimization, denial, and self-medication.

First, minimization... the tendency for people to make their past hurts seem like they're not that big a deal, especially compared to what others have been through. In EMDR therapy circles, we understand that trauma has many faces, and even those things that might be minimized can still be traumatic. To give voice to this reality, we sometimes talk about big "T" trauma and little "t" trauma, recognizing that just because something doesn't fit our expectations of trauma, doesn't mean it isn't traumatic for the person who experienced it.

I've seen people traumatized by war, abuse, natural disasters, and accidents, and most people would recognize these as indeed, traumatic events... but I've also seen people traumatized by neglect, abandonment, ridicule, and smaller traumas that add up over time. In my experience, this "death by a thousand cuts" cumulative effect can be just as damaging, if not more damaging, than a single-event trauma. As mentioned earlier, the course of therapy for someone with a single incident trauma is often shorter than someone with ongoing layers of trauma going back to childhood.

Remember the ACE study I mentioned at the beginning of our course? It's not just physical abuse that can impact us for life... it's the shame, yelling, and neglect. According to the World Health Organization, "It has been shown that considerable and prolonged stress in childhood has lifelong consequences for a person's health and well-being. It can disrupt early brain development and compromise functioning of the nervous and immune systems. In addition, because of the behaviours adopted by some people who have faced ACEs, such stress can lead to serious problems such as alcoholism, depression, eating disorders, unsafe sex, HIV/AIDS, heart disease, cancer, and other chronic diseases."[31]

This study makes it more difficult to minimize childhood trauma, and forces us to confront the reality that our physical and emotional health are inseparable. If you've gone through these things and have convinced yourself that you're doing well, it's important to ask, "at what cost?" What have you had to give up to function? How healthy are your relationships? Sometimes, the very coping skills that get us through childhood and supposedly make us "tough" destroy our lives down the road. Just like a smartphone app, our coping skills need an occasional update. When was the last time your coping skills for life got an update? If you've experienced any Adverse Childhood Experiences, I would suggest giving EMDR therapy a try.

Minimizing the impact of trauma in your life has an advantage. Short term, it allows us to ignore the hard realities connected to our past. To face these things means to open up old wounds, which is uncomfortable. Sometimes we're afraid of what we'll find, or afraid that it will change our relationships. It's

---

[31] World Health Organization Website, https://www.who.int/violence_injury_prevention/violence/activities/adverse_childhood_experiences/en/.

normal to minimize, because it protects us. However, long-term, it doesn't work. The old hurts catch up with us, and the energy it takes to minimize and cope with the deeper issues leads to its own set of problems.

The sad reality is that the majority of people who really need EMDR therapy don't realize it. They don't realize it because in order to cope, their brains have adapted to live with trauma. Back to the earlier analogy of trauma being like a tiger in the cave... some of us get so good at avoiding the tiger... that is, avoiding any person, place, thing, situation, or emotion related to our trauma... that we become masters of avoidance.

Some of us become so good at avoiding our trauma, we're not even aware that we're doing it! Yet, if you take a step back, and take a truly honest look at yourself, you might be surprised at what you find. Some minimize their trauma, and others have convinced themselves that it doesn't even exist. This brings us to the second way of avoiding trauma, denial.

If you suspect that you, or someone you love, might fall into this camp, it's important to dig a little deeper. Or, even if you don't suspect it, it's still important to dig deeper, because if you're in denial, by definition, you don't know it.

"What are the things in life that you try and avoid?"

Imagine if you were sitting in my office right now, wondering if you need EMDR therapy. In addition to taking a good history on your childhood, talking with you about how trauma changes our developing brains, and validating any painful experiences you endured, I would then ask you some questions about your life today. First, I'd ask you

"What are the things in life that you try and avoid?" Think about that one for a moment...

Once you've identified these things, then I'd simply ask you "Why do you avoid them?" If you don't have any trauma, then why the avoidance... why the anxiety... why the fear?

If after exploring this, it turns out that there are some things you're avoiding, it wouldn't make you weak. It would just mean that you're human... a human, doing what humans naturally do after trauma... without necessarily even being conscious of it, we tend to compartmentalize and avoid reminders of the trauma at all costs in order to prevent future pain.

Short term, avoidance works. But as long as the trauma goes unhealed, it continues to be a threat... just one reminder away from poking the tiger and opening the floodgates. I can't tell you how many men will sit in my office and claim they don't have any trauma and aren't avoiding anything. However, their desire to gloss over the conversation, show skepticism, and see the world through "rose colored glasses" are all classic giveaways that they're in avoidance mode. And again I don't blame them... if I were in their shoes I'd probably do the same thing.

"... in most cases our deepest phobia is of a feeling."

When it comes up, I recognize the avoidance for what it is, and I respect it, but I also feel obligated to challenge it… and when I dig a little deeper, the truth usually comes out.

For example, the guy who can't have a calm conversation with his wife about anything that resembles criticism. Instead, he ends up becoming defensive and angry, and either yells or walks out of the house. I explain to him, that like most of us, our deepest phobia isn't about spiders, or heights, or any of the things we typically associate with fear. No, in most cases <u>our deepest phobia is of a feeling</u>… an emotion embedded in a deep insecurity about ourselves.

It might be the feeling of helplessness, or danger. It might be the feeling of being a failure, or being incompetent. Or, it might be feeling unlovable, worthless, or just not good enough. Again, back to the idea of negative cognitions that we talked about earlier... most of us have at least one deep insecurity that we try to avoid, but when we can identify it and acknowledge it, two things can happen. First, it helps explain a lot of our behavior... why we do what we do, why we might be stuck in certain areas, and why certain relationships might not be the healthiest. And second, it highlights our need for EMDR therapy... an opportunity to heal our insecurities at the source, to rip it out by the roots, once and for all. While it's completely natural to cope with trauma by avoiding pain, it's also natural to cope with trauma by seeking things that give us pleasure. This brings us to the third method of avoidance... self-medication.

Self-medication points to our tendency to try and regulate our emotions through pleasurable, and often addictive activities. Common examples include alcohol use, the abuse of either illegal or prescription drugs, sex, pornography use, shopping, gambling, emotional-eating, excessive use of video games, computer, or television, texting, social media, workaholism... the list could go on, but I think you get the idea. If you can identify with one or more of these behaviors, then join the club. We all have pain, and it has to go somewhere. What these behaviors all have in common is their ability to activate the reward systems in our brains and help us experience pleasure. Of course, these highs are short lived and unsustainable. In the long run they only lead to more pain, and unless the underlying insecurities and traumatic experiences are dealt with they will continue to cause problems. Unless you face the tiger inside, it's only a matter of time before it catches up with you.

Concluding Questions

So, in summary, if you're still wondering if you could benefit from EMDR therapy, please reflect on the following questions.

"Have you ever been diagnosed with, or been suspected to have PTSD?"

"Have you ever experienced something that threatened your life, your physical or emotional well-being, or your identity?"

"Have you ever been through one of the adverse childhood experiences specified in the Ace Study?"

"Have you ever had a doctor, pastor, counselor, friend, or loved one mentioned concern about you having posttraumatic stress, addiction, or other unhealthy behavior?"

"Have you shown avoidance behaviors through minimization, denial, or self-medication, or been accused of these behaviors by others?"

"Have you ever experienced severe human suffering, a natural disaster, or an accident?"

"Have you been through military combat or worked as a police officer, firefighter, paramedic, nurse, or doctor?"

"Have you ever experienced physical, emotional, or sexual abuse or assault?"

If you answered yes to any of these questions, there's a good chance you've experienced trauma and would benefit from EMDR therapy. Whether or not you choose to get EMDR therapy is, of course, a very personal decision, and I understand that people approach the idea of therapy in different ways. As mentioned earlier, for some, it's a last resort... something to do reluctantly after a crisis, or after life becomes unmanageable, or when facing an ultimatum from a spouse. However, I hope you don't wait that long. Instead, I'd encourage you to view therapy as a resource that could help you live a healthier life.

Like a healthy diet, exercise, or getting enough sleep, for some, therapy can be one component of an overall plan for health and wholeness. If you're already at a crisis point, EMDR therapy may help stabilize things and assist you in turning things around. However, if you're not in crisis yet, EMDR therapy can still be a wise preventative care measure... a way to be proactive rather than reactive... a way to deal with the core issues before they turn into something that really does become unmanageable.

It's probably pretty obvious at this point, that I'm biased towards EMDR therapy. How could I not be? As someone who provides EMDR therapy every week I've seen it transform lives, over and over again. And as someone who's received EMDR therapy for himself, I know what it's like to be on the other side. I know the vulnerable feeling of starting therapy and confiding in a stranger. I know the anxiety of digging up my past and facing my fears and insecurities. But I also know the healing, the peace, and the transformation that comes with EMDR therapy. EMDR changed my life, both as a client, and as a therapist, and from this perspective I've come to believe that most of us could benefit from it.

No one gets through life unscathed. No matter how great your family was growing up, none of us are immune from pain, from loss, and from heartache. There's just so much we can't control, and through no fault of our own, certain experiences can get stuck. If we get cut, we bleed... and if we experience certain, emotionally-distressing situations in life, we become traumatized. Our brains store the information dysfunctionally, cut off from the truthful perspective we need to heal. But the good news is, there's a therapy out there... EMDR therapy, that actually works! When provided by a trained professional, this research-proven, 8 phase protocol can be life changing. It certainly has been for me, for hundreds of my clients, and for millions of others around the world. I sincerely hope you check it out.

Sincerely,

Mark Odland - MA, LMFT, MDIV
mark@bilateralinnovations.com
www.bilateralinnovations.com

About the Author

Mark Odland, MA, LMFT, MDIV is a Licensed Marriage and Family Therapist practicing in the United States. He is an Approved Supervisor through the MN Board of Marriage and Family Therapy, an EMDRIA-Certified Therapist and Approved Consultant, and an Approved Consultant and Basic Training Facilitator through EMDR-HAP (Trauma Recovery). Mark received his Bachelor of Arts degree from Augustana University in Sioux Falls, South Dakota with a double major in Art and Religion. He went on to receive his Master of Divinity degree from Luther Seminary in St. Paul, Minnesota, and his Master of Arts in Marriage and Family Therapy from Argosy University in Eagan, Minnesota. Mark often provides EMDR Consultation to help therapists either complete their EMDR Basic Training or go on to become EMDRIA Certified. He also provides continuing education courses to therapists around the world, and is the author of the EMDR Coloring Book series.

PURPOSE

Mark founded Bilateral Innovations with the following purpose:

Bilateral Innovations provides Consultation and Continuing Education, for the purpose of transforming the world, one client at a time.

To learn more, please visit his website at: bilateralinnovations.com

OTHER BOOKS BY MARK INCLUDE:

- The EMDR Coloring Book: A Calming Resource for Adults Featuring 200 Works of Fine Art Paired with 200 Positive Affirmations

- The EMDR Coloring Book II: A Calming Resource for Adults Featuring 100 Works of Art Paired with 100 Positive Affirmations

- The EMDR Coloring Book for Kids: A Resource for Therapists, Parents, and Children

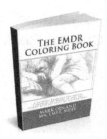  

Made in the USA
Coppell, TX
28 February 2020